# GOOD DOG, MILLIE

# Story by Andy Mayer and Jim Becker ★ Illustrations by Mary Kittilä

Macmillan Publishing Company
*New York*

★

Maxwell Macmillan Canada
*Toronto*

★

Maxwell Macmillan International
*New York   Oxford   Singapore   Sydney*

*To my three special boys — Robert, Jari and Jackson — all my love
and thanks for your help and patience. Couldn't have done it without you!
And to Andy and Jim — wouldn't have done it without you! Many, many thanks.*

M.K.

*Endpaper Art by Skeezix*

**Copyright © 1992 by Jim Becker and Andy Mayer**

Macmillan Publishing Company
866 Third Avenue
New York, NY 10022

Maxwell Macmillan Canada, Inc.
1200 Eglinton Avenue East,
Suite 200
Don Mills, Ontario M3C 3N1

Macmillan Publishing Company is part of
the Maxwell Communication Group of Companies.

**Library of Congress Cataloging-in-Publication Data**

Becker, Jim
    Good Dog, Millie: a day in the life of America's
most influential canine / Jim Becker, Andy Mayer,
Mary Kittilä.

        p.    cm.
    ISBN 0-02-508201-9
    1. Millie (Dog) 2. Bush, George. 1924-  3. Bush,
Barbara. 1925-  4. Dogs — United States —
Biography. I. Mayer, Andrew. 1954-  II. Kittilä,
Mary. III. Title.

    E882.2.B44        1993        92-9152 CIP
    973.928' 092' 2 — dc20

Macmillan books are available at special discounts for bulk
purchases for sales promotions, premiums, fund-raising, or
educational use. For details, contact:

Special Sales Director
Macmillan Publishing Company
866 Third Avenue
New York, NY 10022

*Good Dog, Millie* is produced by **becker&mayer!**

10  9  8  7  6  5  4  3  2  1
Printed in the United States of America

"Look after George, Millie.
I'll be back at five."

"Good dog, Millie!"

# The End